My Special Place

Pilawuk White

Illustrated by Vasja Koman

My name is Niwili.
It is school holiday time.
This is a special time away
from my home in the city.

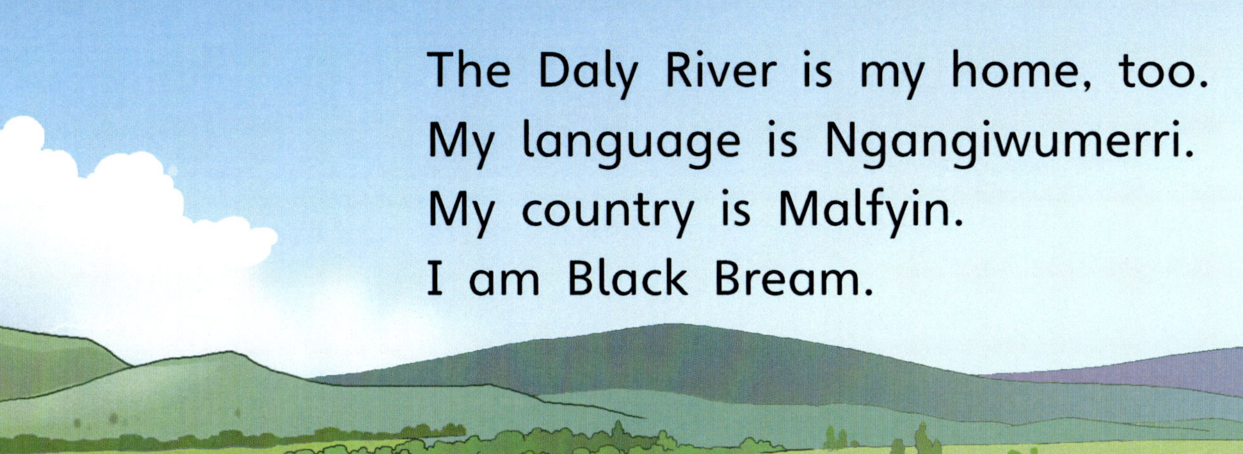

The Daly River is my home, too.
My language is Ngangiwumerri.
My country is Malfyin.
I am Black Bream.

Fish River is my Uncle Shotgun's country.
He always takes me fishing.
We pack the tinny.

We leave at first light.
We drive on a dirt road and then on sand.
We cross over a bridge.
At sunrise we get to the turn off.

We fish at the billabong.
There are birds, fish ... and even crocodiles.
I feel safe in Uncle Shotgun's tinny.

I catch a Black Bream.
Black Bream is special to me.
I must not hurt it.
I place the fish back in the water.

We catch a big barramundi.
This fish is for my Aunty.

I see a log above the water.
"Uncle Shotgun, is that a log or a crocodile?"

The crocodile snaps at our tinny.
Uncle Shotgun pokes it in the eye.
The crocodile is gone.

Last light tells us it is time to go home.

Back home in the city, I go to school.
I think of my special place.
I am Black Bream.
I am Niwili.